THE MEDITE
DIET COO~~KBOOK~~
–
MEAT, PORK, AND POULTRY EDITION

Mouthwatering and Amazingly Easy Recipes to Fry, Bake, Grill, and Roast using the Healthy Mediterranean Method

Erica Whitman

for any hardship or damages that may befall them after undertaking information described herein.

Additionally, the information in the following pages is intended only for informational purposes and should thus be thought of as universal. As befitting its nature, it is presented without assurance regarding its prolonged validity or interim quality. Trademarks that are mentioned are done without written consent and can in no way be considered an endorsement from the trademark holder.

Table of Contents

INTRODUCTION

Bring the Mediterranean--from Italy and Greece to Morocco and Egypt, to Turkey and Lebanon--into your kitchen with many fresh, flavorful recipes.

From southern Italy, Sardinia, and France to Spain, Greece, and Northern Africa, the Mediterranean regions are synonymous with sparkling azure waters and clear blue skies. It's also home to most of the world's longest-lived and vibrantly healthy people. Now we know why! Repeatedly ranked the #1 diet by U.S. News and World Report...So, Meat, Pork, and Poultry enthusiasts unite!

This book has you covered from the basic to the spectacular with recipes that deliver low-key dinners, game-day favorites, simple burgers, special-occasion showstoppers, and beyond using the "Mediterranean Method."

You can call chicken or pork or beef a lot of things. A blank canvas, weeknight go-to, lean protein, we've heard it all. But boring? That's where we draw the line. Sure, it might have started to feel a bit redundant. But that's not the pork or beef or chicken's fault. This book is here with the inspiration you need. It's time those pork and chicken pieces in your freezer got the respect they deserve.

Chicken, for instance, is the go-anywhere, eat-with-anything, a highly transformable crowd favorite that always fills the bill. Find exactly what you're looking for with a wide breadth of themed recipes, including Easy Dinners, Classic Braises, Breaded and Fried, Casseroles, and appliance-specific recipes.

MEAT, PORK, AND POULTRY RECIPES

Beef & Broccoli

Preparation Time: 15 minutes

Cooking Time: 15 minutes

Servings: 4

Ingredients:

2 tablespoons peanut oil

2 cloves garlic, chopped

8 oz. sirloin beef, sliced into strips

4 cups broccoli, sliced into florets

1/4 cup low-sodium chicken broth

1 tablespoon cornstarch

2 tablespoons low-sodium soy sauce

2 cups cooked white rice

Directions:

Heat oil in a pan over medium heat.

Cook the garlic for 30 seconds.

Add the broccoli and cook for 5 minutes.

Remove and set aside.

Add the beef and cook for 7 minutes.

Combine broth, soy sauce and cornstarch in a bowl.

Put the broccoli back to the pan.

Add the sauce and simmer until the sauce has thickened.

Serve with rice.

Nutrition:

Calories 373

Protein 18 g

Carbohydrates 37 g

Fat 17 g

Cholesterol 42 mg

Sodium 351 mg

Potassium 555 mg

Phosphorus 255 mg

Calcium 62 mg

Fiber 5.1 g

Baked Pork Chops

Preparation Time: 15 minutes

Cooking Time: 40 minutes

Servings: 6

Ingredients:

1/2 cup all-purpose flour

1 egg, beaten

1/4 cup water

3/4 cup cornflake crumbs

6 pork chops

2 tablespoons butter

1 teaspoon paprika

Directions:

Preheat your oven to 350 degrees F.

Put flour in a plate.

In a bowl, mix egg and water.

Add cornflakes in another bowl.

Coat each pork chop with flour, dip in the egg mixture and dredge with cornflakes.

Drizzle melted butter on top.

Sprinkle paprika on top of the butter.

Bake in the oven for 40 minutes.

Nutrition:

Calories 282

Protein 23 g

Carbohydrates 25 g

Fat 10 g

Cholesterol 95 mg

Sodium 263 mg

Potassium 394 mg

Phosphorus 203 mg

Calcium 28 mg

Fiber 1.4 g

Balsamic Pork Chops

Preparation Time: 10 minutes

Cooking Time: 20 minutes

Servings: 4

Ingredients:

4 pork chops, trimmed

3 tablespoons balsamic vinegar

1/2 teaspoon dried thyme

1/2 teaspoon dried rosemary

1/4 teaspoon garlic powder

1/4 teaspoon black pepper

2 tablespoons vegetable oil

1 teaspoon unsalted butter

4 oz. mushrooms, sliced

1 onion, sliced

Directions:

Coat pork chops with vinegar and season with herbs and spices.

Pour oil into a pan over medium heat.

Cook pork chops for 6 minutes.

Turn the pork chops and reduce heat.

Cover and cook for 10 minutes.

Transfer pork on a plate.

Add the butter, mushrooms and onions.

Cook for 2 minutes.

Pour the onion and mushroom with cooking liquid on top of the pork chops before serving.

Nutrition:

Calories 285

Protein 28 g

Carbohydrates 5 g

Fat 17 g

Cholesterol 81 mg

Sodium 79 mg

Potassium 560 mg

Phosphorus 274 mg

Calcium 40 mg

Fiber 0.7 g

Braised Beef

Preparation Time: 20 minutes

Cooking Time: 1 hour and 30 minutes

Servings: 8

Ingredients:

2 lb. beef brisket, trimmed

2 teaspoons black pepper

2 tablespoons olive oil

1/2 onion, chopped

1 carrot, sliced

1 stalk celery, chopped

3 bay leaves, crumbled

1 tablespoon fresh parsley, chopped

2 cups low-sodium beef broth

3 cups water

2 tablespoons balsamic vinegar

Directions:

Preheat your oven to 350 degrees F.

Season beef with black pepper.

Pour oil in a pot and brown the meat for 5 minutes per side.

Transfer meat to a plate and add onion, carrot and celery.

Cook for 4 minutes.

Add bay leaves and parsley.

Put the meat on top of the veggies.

Add the rest of the ingredients.

Cover and bring to a boil.

Transfer contents of pot to baking pan.

Bake in the oven for 1 hour.

Nutrition:

Calories 230

Protein 29 g

Carbohydrates 4 g

Fat 11 g

Cholesterol 84 mg

Sodium 178 mg

Potassium 346 mg

Phosphorus 193 mg

Calcium 30 mg

Fiber 0.8 g

Pork Loins with Leeks

Preparation Time: 10 minutes

Cooking Time: 35 minutes

Servings: 2

Ingredients:

1 sliced leek

1 tablespoon mustard seeds

6-ounce Pork tenderloin

1 tablespoon cumin seeds

1 tablespoon dry mustard

1 tablespoon extra-virgin oil

Directions:

Preheat the broiler to medium high heat.

In a dry skillet heat mustard and cumin seeds until they start to pop (3-5 minutes).

Grind seeds using a pestle and mortar or blender and then mix in the dry mustard.

Coat the pork on both sides with the mustard blend and add to a baking tray to broil for 25-30 minutes or until cooked through. Turn once halfway through.

Remove and place to one side.

Heat the oil in a pan on medium heat and add the leeks for 5-6 minutes or until soft.

Serve the pork tenderloin on a bed of leeks and enjoy!

Nutrition:

Calories 139

Fat 5g

Carbs 2g

Phosphorus 278mg

Potassium (K) 45mg

Sodium (Na) 47mg

Protein 18g

Chinese Beef Wraps

Preparation Time: 10 minutes

Cooking Time: 30 minutes

Servings: 2

Ingredients:

2 iceberg lettuce leaves

½ diced cucumber

1 teaspoon canola oil

5-ounce lean ground beef

1 teaspoon ground ginger

1 tablespoon chili flakes

1 minced garlic clove

1 tablespoon rice wine vinegar

Directions:

Mix the ground meat with the garlic, rice wine vinegar, chili flakes and ginger in a bowl.

Heat oil in a skillet over medium heat.

Add the beef to the pan and cook for 20-25 minutes or until cooked through.

Serve beef mixture with diced cucumber in each lettuce wrap and fold.

Nutrition:

Calories 156

Fat 2g Carbs 4 g

Phosphorus 1 mg

Sodium (Na) 54mg

Protein 14g

California Pork Chops

Preparation Time: 10 minutes

Cooking Time: 10 minutes

Total time: 20 minutes

Servings: 2

Ingredients:

1 tbsp fresh cilantro, chopped

1/2 cup chives, chopped

2 large green bell peppers, chopped

1 lb 1" thick boneless pork chops

1 tbsp fresh lime juice

2 cups cooked rice

1/8 tsp dried oregano leaves

1/4 tsp ground black pepper

1/4 tsp ground cumin

1 tbsp butter

1 lime

Directions:

Start by seasoning the pork chops with lime juice and cilantro. Place them in a shallow dish.

Toss the chives with pepper, cumin, butter, oregano and rice in a bowl.

Stuff the bell peppers with this mixture and place them around the pork chops.

Cover the chop and bell peppers with a foil sheet and bake them for 10 minutes in the oven at 375 degrees F.

Serve warm.

Nutrition:

Calories 265.

Protein 34 g.

Carbohydrates 24 g.

Fat 15 g.

Cholesterol 86 mg.

Sodium 70 mg.

Potassium 564 mg.

Phosphorus 240 mg.

Calcium 22 mg.

Fiber 1.0 g.

Beef Chorizo

Preparation Time: 10 minutes

Cooking Time: 10 minutes

Total time: 20 minutes

Servings: 4

Ingredients:

3 garlic cloves, minced

1 lb 90% lean ground beef

2 tbsp hot chili powder

2 tsp red or cayenne pepper

1 tsp black pepper

1 tsp ground oregano

2 tsp white vinegar

Directions:

Mix all ingredients together in a bowl thoroughly then spread the mixture in a baking pan.

Bake the meat for 10 minutes at 325 degrees F in an oven.

Slice and serve in crumbles.

Nutrition:

Calories 72.

Protein 8 g.

Carbohydrates 1 g.

Fat 4 g.

Cholesterol 25 mg.

Sodium 46 mg.

Potassium 174 mg.

Phosphorus 79 mg.

Calcium 14 mg.

Fiber 0.8 g.

Pork Fajitas

Preparation Time: 10 minutes

Cooking Time: 20 minutes

Servings: 4

Ingredients:

1 green bell pepper, julienned

1 medium onion, julienned

2 garlic cloves, minced

1 lb lean, boneless pork cut into strips

1 tsp dried oregano

1/2 tsp cumin

2 tbsp pineapple juice

2 tbsp vinegar

1/4 tsp hot pepper sauce

1 tbsp canola oil

4 flour tortillas, 8" size

Directions:

Start by mixing the oregano, garlic, vinegar, cumin, hot sauce, and pineapple juice in a bowl.

Place the pork in this marinade and mix well to coat them then refrigerate for 15 minutes.

Meanwhile, preheat the oven to 325 degrees F.

Wrap the tortillas in a foil and heat them in the oven 2-3 minutes.

Now, heat a suitable griddle on medium heat and add pork strips, green peppers, oil, and onion.

Cook for 5 minutes until pork is done.

Serve warm in warmed tortillas.

Nutrition:

Calories 406.

Protein 26 g.

Carbohydrates 34 g.

Fat 18 g.

Cholesterol 64 mg.

Sodium 376 mg.

Potassium 483 mg.

Phosphorus 267 mg.

Calcium 57 mg.

Fiber 2.4 g.

Herbed Pork Chops

Preparation Time: 15 minutes

Cooking Time: 15 minutes

Servings: 4

Ingredients:

4 pork chops

1 tablespoon fresh lime juice

1 tablespoon fresh cilantro, chopped

1/2 cup chives, chopped

2 green bell peppers, sliced into strips

1/8 teaspoon dried oregano leaves

1/4 teaspoon ground black pepper

1 tablespoon butter, melted

1/4 teaspoon ground cumin

1 tablespoon olive oil

1 lime

Directions:

Coat pork chops with lime juice.

Season with cilantro.

Mix the oregano, pepper, butter and cumin.

Pour oil into a pan over medium heat.

Add the pork chops and cook for 4 minutes per side.

Add the oregano mixture and bell pepper.

Cook for 3 minutes.

Nutrition:

Calories 265

Protein 34 g

Carbohydrates 24 g

Fat 15 g

Cholesterol 86 mg

Sodium 70 mg

Potassium 564 mg

Phosphorus 240 mg

Calcium 22 mg

Fiber 1.0 g

Dijon Pork Chops

Preparation Time: 15 minutes

Cooking Time: 15 minutes

Servings: 4

Ingredients:

4 pork loin chops

2 tablespoons all-purpose flour

1/4 cup shallots, chopped

2 teaspoons fresh ginger root, grated

1 tablespoon butter

1/2 cup low-sodium chicken broth

2 tablespoons dry sherry

2 teaspoons Dijon mustard

1 teaspoon mustard seed

1/8 teaspoon pepper

Parsley

Directions:

Coat both sides of pork chops with flour.

In a pan over medium heat, add the butter and cook pork chops until golden brown.

Place on a platter and keep warm.

Add sherry and broth to the skillet.

Bring to a boil.

Lower heat.

Add the shallots and ginger root.

Cook for 2 minutes.

Add the rest of the ingredients.

Pour the sauce over the pork chops before serving.

Nutrition:

Calories 296

Protein 27 g

Carbohydrates 5 g

Fat 17 g

Cholesterol 78 mg

Sodium 168 mg

Potassium 438 mg

Phosphorus 248 mg

Calcium 34 mg

Fiber 0.5 g

Barbecue Beef

Preparation Time: 10 minutes

Cooking Time: 5 hours

Servings: 14

Ingredients:

3/4 cup brown sugar

12 oz. beer

8 oz. ketchup

4 lb. chuck roast

14 hamburger buns

Directions:

Preheat your oven to 325 degrees F.

Combine beer, brown sugar and ketchup.

Add the roast in a baking pan.

Coat with the mixture.

Cover with foil.

Bake for 5 hours.

Slice meat or shred using a fork.

Serve on buns.

Nutrition:

Calories 450

Protein 33 g

Carbohydrates 32 g

Fat 21 g

Cholesterol 92 mg

Sodium 261 mg

Potassium 357 mg

Phosphorus 207 mg

Calcium 85 mg

Fiber 0.6 g

Pork Souvlaki

Preparation Time: 1 hour

Cooking Time: 15 minutes

Servings: 6

Ingredients:

3 tablespoons lemon juice

1/4 cup olive oil

1/8 teaspoon black pepper

1 teaspoon dried oregano

1 lb. pork tenderloin, cubed

1 onion, sliced

2 cloves garlic, minced

1 bell green pepper, sliced

Directions:

In a bowl, combine lemon juice, oil, pepper and oregano.

Marinate pork cubes in the mixture for 45 minutes inside the refrigerator.

Thread the pork, onion and bell pepper into skewers.

Grill for 15 minutes, turning halfway through.

Serve with rice or salad.

Nutrition:

Calories 204

Protein 18 g

Carbohydrates 5 g

Fat 13 g

Cholesterol 53 mg

Sodium 58 mg

Potassium 336 mg

Phosphorus 179 mg

Calcium 17 mg

Fiber 0 g

Roasted Lamb

Preparation Time: 30 minutes

Cooking Time: 1 hour and 30 minutes

Servings: 10

Ingredients:

1/4 cup fresh rosemary leaves

2 tablespoons dried oregano

1 teaspoon black pepper

2 garlic cloves, minced

4 tablespoons butter, divided

1 leg of lamb, trimmed

1/4 cup fresh lemon juice

1 cup water

Directions:

Preheat your oven to 325 degrees F.

In a bowl, combine the rosemary, oregano, pepper and garlic.

Stir in 2 tablespoons butter.

Create slits on both sides of the lamb using a sharp knife.

Stuff these slits with herb and butter mixture.

Coat the lamb with the remaining mixture.

Cover with foil and bake for 1 hour.

Uncover the lamb and bake for another 30 minutes.

Nutrition:

Calories 318

Protein 30 g

Carbohydrates 0 g

Fat 22 g

Cholesterol 118 mg

Sodium 114 mg

Potassium 394 mg

Phosphorus 228 mg

Calcium 32 mg

Fiber 0.5 g

Italian Beef

Preparation Time: 30 minutes

Cooking Time: 5 hours and 45 minutes

Servings: 15

Ingredients:

3 lb. lean beef roast, trimmed

2 teaspoons oregano

2 teaspoons black pepper

1 teaspoon garlic powder

1 teaspoon red pepper, crushed

1 onion, sliced

1 green bell pepper, sliced

1 yellow bell pepper, sliced

1 red bell pepper, sliced

1/2 cup pepperoncini juice

Directions:

Put all the ingredients except the bell peppers, onion and pepperoncini juice in a slow cooker.

Cook on high setting for 5 hours.

Shred beef and put it back to the pot.

Add the rest of the ingredients.

Cook on high setting for 45 minutes.

Nutrition:

Calories 212

Protein 25 g

Carbohydrates 3 g

Fat 11 g

Cholesterol 84 mg

Sodium 121 mg

Potassium 280 mg

Phosphorus 196 mg

Calcium 21 mg

Fiber 0.6 g

Meat & Rice Balls

Preparation Time: 15 minutes

Cooking Time: 40 minutes

Servings: 4

Ingredients:

1 lb. lean ground beef

4 cups cooked white rice

1 egg

3/4 teaspoon herb seasoning blend

2 1/4 cups water

Directions:

Mix the beef, rice and egg.

Roll and form 24 balls.

Cook the balls in a pan over medium heat.

Mix the herb seasoning and water.

Add the mixture to the pan.

Bring to a boil and then reduce heat and simmer covered for 30 minutes.

Nutrition:

Calories 348

Protein 24 g

Carbohydrates 18 g

Fat 20 g

Cholesterol 131 mg

Sodium 95 mg

Potassium 350 mg

Phosphorus 197 mg

Calcium 21 mg

Fiber 0.5 g

Shish Kebabs

Preparation Time: 40 minutes

Cooking Time: 30 minutes

Servings: 6

Ingredients:

1/2 cup olive oil

1/2 cup white vinegar

1/4 teaspoon garlic powder

1/2 teaspoon oregano

1/4 teaspoon black pepper

1 1/2 pounds beef sirloin, cubed

2 onions, sliced

2 green bell peppers, sliced

1 red bell pepper, sliced

Directions:

Combine oil, vinegar, garlic powder, oregano and pepper in a bowl.

Soak the beef cubes in the marinade for 30 minutes.

Thread beef cubes and vegetables into the skewers.

Grill for 30 minutes.

Nutrition:

Calories 358

Protein 26 g

Carbohydrates 5 g

Fat 26 g

Cholesterol 80 mg

Sodium 60 mg

Potassium 458 mg

Phosphorus 217 mg

Calcium 25 mg

Fiber 1.4 g

Beef Chili

Preparation Time: 10 minutes

Cooking Time: 30 minutes

Servings: 2

Ingredients:

Onion – 1, diced

Red bell pepper – 1, diced

Garlic – 2 cloves, minced

Lean ground beef – 6 oz.

Chili powder – 1 tsp.

Oregano – 1 tsp.

Extra virgin olive oil – 2 Tbsps.

Water – 1 cup

Brown rice -1 cup

Fresh cilantro – 1 Tbsp. to serve

Directions:

Soak vegetables in warm water.

Bring a pan of water to the boil and add rice for 20 minutes.

Meanwhile, add the oil to a pan and heat on medium-high heat.

Add the pepper, onions, and garlic and sauté for 5 minutes until soft.

Remove and set aside.

Add the beef to the pan and stir until browned.

Add the vegetables back into the pan and stir.

Now add the chili powder and herbs and the water, cover and turn the heat down a little to simmer for 15 minutes.

Meanwhile, drain the water from the rice, and the lid and steam while the chili is cooking.

Serve hot with the fresh cilantro sprinkled over the top.

Nutrition:

Calories: 459

Fat: 22g

Carb: 36g

Phosphorus: 332mg

Potassium: 360mg

Sodium: 33mg

Protein: 22g

Roast Beef

Preparation Time: 25 minutes

Cooking Time: 55 minutes

Servings: 3

Ingredients:

Quality rump or sirloin tip roast

Directions:

Place in roasting pan o n a shallow rack

Season with pepper and herbs

Insert meat thermometer in the center or thickest part of the roast

Roast to the desired degree of doneness

After removing from over for about 15 minutes let it chill

In the end the roast should be moister than well done.

Nutrition:

Calories 158

Protein 24 g

Fat 6 g

Carbs 0 g

Phosphorus 206 mg

Potassium (K) 328 mg

Sodium (Na) 55 mg

Beef Brochettes

Preparation Time: 20 minutes

Cooking Time: 1 hour

Servings: 1

Ingredients:

1 ½ cups pineapple chunks

1 sliced large onion

2 pounds thick steak

1 sliced medium bell pepper

1 bay leaf

¼ cup vegetable oil

½ cup lemon juice

2 crushed garlic cloves

Directions:

Cut beef cubes and place in a plastic bag

Combine marinade ingredients in small bowl

Mix and pour over beef cubes

Seal the bag and refrigerate for 3 to 5 hours

Divide ingredients onion, beef cube, green pepper, pineapple

Grill about 9 minutes each side

Nutrition:

Calories 304

Protein 35 g

Fat 15 g

Carbs 11 g

Phosphorus 264 mg

Potassium (K) 388 mg

Sodium (Na) 70 mg

Country Fried Steak

Preparation Time: 10 minutes

Cooking Time: 1 hour and 40 minutes

Servings: 3

Ingredients:

1 large onion

½ cup flour

3 tablespoons. vegetable oil

¼ teaspoon pepper

1½ pounds round steak

½ teaspoon paprika

Directions:

Trim excess fat from steak.

Cut into small pieces.

Combine flour, paprika and pepper and mix together.

Preheat skillet with oil.

Cook steak on both sides.

When the color of steak is brown remove to a platter,

Add water (150 ml) and stir around the skillet,

Return browned steak to skillet, if necessary, add water again so that bottom side of steak does not stick.

Nutrition:

Calories 248

Protein 30 g

Fat 10 g

Carbs 5 g

Phosphorus 190 mg

Potassium (K) 338 mg

Sodium (Na) 60 mg

Homemade Burgers

Preparation Time: 10 minutes

Cooking Time: 20 minutes

Servings: 2

Ingredients:

4 ounce lean 100% ground beef

1 teaspoon black pepper

1 garlic clove, minced

1 teaspoon olive oil

1/4 cup onion, finely diced

1 tablespoon balsamic vinegar

1/2ounce brie cheese, crumbled

1 teaspoon mustard

Directions:

Season ground beef with pepper and then mix in minced garlic.

Form burger shapes with the ground beef using the palms of your hands.

Heat a skillet on a medium to high heat, and then add the oil.

Sauté the onions for 5-10 minutes until browned.

Then add the balsamic vinegar and sauté for another 5 minutes.

Remove and set aside.

Add the burgers to the pan and heat on the same heat for 5-6 minutes before flipping and heating for a further 5-6 minutes until cooked through.

Spread the mustard onto each burger.

Crumble the brie cheese over each burger and serve!

Try with a crunchy side salad!

Tip: If using fresh beef and not defrosted, prepare double the ingredients and freeze burgers in plastic wrap (after cooling) for up to 1 month.

Thoroughly defrost before heating through completely in the oven to serve.

Nutrition:

Calories: 178

Fat: 10g

Carbohydrates: 4g

Phosphorus: 147mg

Potassium: 272mg

Sodium: 273 mg

Protein: 16g

Slow-cooked Beef Brisket

Preparation Time: 10 minutes

Cooking Time: 3 hours and 30 minutes

Servings: 6

Ingredients:

10-ounce chuck roast

1 onion, sliced

1 cup carrots, peeled and sliced

1 tablespoon mustard

1 tablespoon thyme (fresh or dried)

1 tablespoon rosemary (fresh or dried)

2 garlic cloves

2 tablespoon extra-virgin olive oil

1 teaspoon black pepper

1 cup homemade chicken stock (p.52)

1 cup water

Directions:

Preheat oven to 300°f/150°c/Gas Mark 2.

Trim any fat from the beef and soak vegetables in warm water.

Make a paste by mixing together the mustard, thyme, rosemary, and garlic, before mixing in the oil and pepper.

Combine this mix with the stock.

Pour the mixture over the beef into an oven proof baking dish.

Place the vegetables onto the bottom of the baking dish with the beef.

Cover and roast for 3 hours, or until tender.

Uncover the dish and continue to cook for 30 minutes in the oven.

Serve hot!

Nutrition:

Calories: 151 Fat: 7g

Carbohydrates: 7g

Phosphorus: 144mg

Potassium: 344mg

Sodium: 279mg

Protein: 15g

Beef and Three Pepper Stew

Preparation Time: 15 minutes

Cooking Time: 6 hours

Servings: 6

Ingredients:

10ounce of flat cut beef brisket, whole

1 teaspoon of dried thyme

1 teaspoon of black pepper

1 clove garlic

½ cup of green onion, thinly sliced

½ cup low sodium chicken stock

2 cups water

1 large green bell pepper, sliced

1 large red bell pepper, sliced

1 large yellow bell pepper, sliced

1 large red onion, sliced

Directions:

Combine the beef, thyme, pepper, garlic, green onion, stock and water in a slow cooker.

Leave it all to cook on High for 4-5 hours until tender.

Remove the beef from the slow cooker and let it cool.

Shred the beef with two forks and remove any excess fat.

Place the shredded beef back into the slow cooker.

Add the sliced peppers and the onion.

Cook this on High heat for 40-60 minutes until the vegetables are tender.

Nutrition:

Calories: 132

Protein: 14g

Carbohydrates: 9g

Fat: 5g

Cholesterol: 39mg

Sodium: 179mg

Potassium: 390mg

Phosphorus: 141mg

Calcium: 33mg

Fiber: 2g

Sticky Pulled Beef Open Sandwiches

Preparation Time: 15 minutes

Cooking Time: 5 hours

Servings: 5

Ingredients:

½ cup of green onion, sliced

2 garlic cloves

2 tablespoons of fresh parsley

2 large carrots

7ounce of flat cut beef brisket, whole

1 tablespoon of smoked paprika

1 teaspoon dried parsley

1 teaspoon of brown sugar

½ teaspoon of black pepper

2 tablespoon of olive oil

¼ cup of red wine

8 tablespoon of cider vinegar

3 cups of water

5 slices white bread

1 cup of arugula to garnish

Directions:

Finely chop the green onion, garlic and fresh parsley.

Grate the carrot.

Put the beef in to roast in a slow cooker.

Add the chopped onion, garlic and remaining ingredients, leaving the rolls, fresh parsley and arugula to one side.

Stir in the slow cooker to combine.

Cover and cook on Low for 8 1/2 to 10 hours, or on High for 4 to 5 hours until tender. (Hint: Test for tenderness by pressing into the meat with a fork.)

Remove the meat from the slow cooker.

Shred it apart with two forks.

Return the meat to the broth to keep it warm until ready to serve.

Lightly toast the bread and top with shredded beef, arugula, fresh parsley and ½ spoon of the broth.

Serve.

Nutrition:

Calories: 273

Protein: 15g

Carbohydrates: 20g

Fat: 11g

Cholesterol: 37mg

Sodium: 308mg

Potassium: 399mg

Phosphorus: 159mg

Calcium: 113mg

Fiber: 3g

Herby Beef Stroganoff and Fluffy Rice

Preparation Time: 15 minutes

Cooking Time: 5 hours

Servings: 6

Ingredients:

½ cup onion

2 garlic cloves

9ounce of flat cut beef brisket, cut into 1" cubes

½ cup of reduced-sodium beef stock

1/3 cup red wine

½ teaspoon dried oregano

¼ teaspoon freshly ground black pepper

½ teaspoon dried thyme

½ teaspoon of saffron

½ cup almond milk (unenriched)

¼ cup all-purpose flour

1 cup of water

2 ½ cups of white rice

Directions:

Chop up the onion and mince the garlic cloves.

Mix the beef, stock, wine, onion, garlic, oregano, pepper, thyme and saffron in your slow cooker.

Cover and cook on High until the beef is tender, for about 4-5 hours.

Combine the almond milk, flour and water.

Whisk together until smooth.

Add the flour mixture to the slow cooker.

Cook for another 15 to 25 minutes until the stroganoff is thick.

Cook the rice using the package instructions, leaving out salt.

Drain off the excess water.

Serve the stroganoff over the rice.

Nutrition:

Calories: 241

Protein: 15g

Carbohydrates: 29g

Fat: 5g

Cholesterol: 39g

Sodium: 182mg

Potassium: 206mg

Phosphorus: 151mg

Calcium: 59mg

Chunky Beef and Potato Slow Roast

Preparation Time: 15 minutes

Cooking Time: 5-6 hours

Servings: 12

Ingredients:

3 cups of peeled potatoes, chunked

1 cup of onion

2 garlic cloves, chopped

1 ¼ pounds flat cut beef brisket, fat trimmed

2 of cups water

1 teaspoon of chili powder

1 tablespoon of dried rosemary

For the sauce:

1 tablespoon of freshly grated horseradish

½ cup of almond milk (unenriched)

1 tablespoon lemon juice (freshly squeezed)

1 garlic clove, minced

A pinch of cayenne pepper

Directions:

Double boil the potatoes to reduce their potassium content.
(Hint: Bring your potato to the boil, then drain and refill with
water to boil again.)

Chop the onion and the garlic.

Place the beef brisket in slow cooker.

Combine water, chopped garlic, chili powder and rosemary

Pour the mixture over the brisket.

Cover and cook on High for 4-5 hours until the meat is very tender.

Drain the potatoes and add them to the slow cooker.

Turn heat to High and cook covered until the potatoes are tender.

Prepare the horseradish sauce by whisking together horseradish, milk, lemon juice, minced garlic and cayenne pepper.

Cover and refrigerate.

Serve your casserole with a dash of horseradish sauce on the side.

Nutrition:

Calories: 199

Protein: 21g

Carbohydrates: 12g

Fat: 7g

Cholesterol: 63mg

Sodium: 282mg

Potassium: 317

Phosphorus: 191mg

Calcium: 23mg

Fiber: 1g

Beef Pot Roast

Preparation Time: 20 minutes

Cooking Time: 1 hour

Servings: 3

Ingredients:

Round bone roast

2 - 4 pounds chuck roast

Directions:

Trim off excess fat.

Place a tablespoon of oil in a large skillet and heat to medium.

Roll pot roast in flour and brown on all sides in a hot skillet.

After the meat gets a brown color, reduce heat to low.

Season with pepper and herbs and add ½ cup of water.

Cook slowly for 1½ hours or until it looks ready.

Nutrition:

Calories 157

Protein 24 g

Fat 13 g

Carbs 0 g

Phosphorus 204 mg

Sodium (Na) 50 mg

Mouthwatering Beef and Chili Stew

Preparation Time: 15 minutes

Cooking Time: 7 hours

Servings: 6

Ingredients:

1/2 medium red onion, thinly sliced into half moons

1/2 tablespoon vegetable oil

10ounce of flat cut beef brisket, whole

½ cup low sodium stock

¾ cup water

½ tablespoon honey

½ tablespoon chili powder

½ teaspoon smoked paprika

½ teaspoon dried thyme

1 teaspoon black pepper

1 tablespoon corn starch

Directions:

Throw the sliced onion into the slow cooker first.

Add a splash of oil to a large hot skillet and briefly seal the beef on all sides.

Remove the beef from skillet and place in the slow cooker.

Add the stock, water, honey and spices to the same skillet that you cooked the beef in.

Loosen the browned bits from bottom of pan with spatula. (Hint: These brown bits at the bottom are called the fond.)

Allow juice to simmer until the volume is reduced by about half.

Pour the juice over beef in the slow cooker.

Set slow cooker on Low and cook for approximately 7 hours.

Take the beef out of the slow cooker and onto a platter.

Shred it with two forks.

Pour the remaining juice into a medium saucepan. Bring to a simmer.

Whisk the cornstarch with two tablespoons of water.

Add to the juice and cook until slightly thickened.

For a thicker sauce, simmer and reduce the juice a bit more before adding cornstarch.

Pour the sauce over the meat and serve.

Nutrition:

Calories: 128

Protein: 13g

Carbohydrates: 6g

Fat: 6g

Cholesterol: 39mg

Sodium: 228mg

Potassium: 202mg

Phosphorus: 119mg

Calcium: 16mg

Fiber: 1g

Buttery Herb Lamb Chops

Preparation time: 10 minutes.

Cooking Time: 10 Minutes.

Serving: 4.

Ingredients:

- 8 Lamb Chops.
- 1 Tablespoon Olive Oil.
- 1 Tablespoon Butter.
- Sea Salt & Black Pepper to Taste.
- 4 Ounces Herb Butter.
- 1 Lemon, Cut Into Wedges.

Directions:

1. Season your lamb chops with salt and pepper, and then get out a pan.
2. Melt your butter in a pan over medium-high heat and then fry your chops for four minutes per side.
3. Arrange on a serving plate with herb butter on each one. Serve with a lemon wedge.

Nutrition:

Calories: 729.

Protein: 43 Grams.

Fat: 62 Grams.

Carbs: 0.3 Grams.

Kale Chicken Soup

Preparation time: 12 minutes.

Cooking Time: 18 Minutes.

Serving: 6.

Ingredients:

- 1 Tablespoon Olive Oil.
- 3 Cups Kale, Chopped.
- 1 Cup Carrot, Minced.
- 2 Cloves Garlic, Minced.
- 8 Cups Chicken Broth, Low Sodium.
- Sea Salt & Black Pepper to Taste.

- ¾ Cup Patina Pasta, Uncooked.
- 2 Cups Chicken, Cooked & Shredded.
- 3 Tablespoons Parmesan Cheese, Grated.

Directions:

1. Start by getting out a stockpot over medium heat and heat your oil. Add in your garlic, cooking for half a minute. Stir frequently and add in the kale and carrots. Cook for an additional five minutes, and make sure to stir so it doesn't burn.

2. Add in salt, pepper, and broth, turning the heat to high. Bring it to a boil before adding in your pasta.

3. Low the heat to medium, and cook for another ten minutes. Your pasta should be cooked all the way through, but make sure to stir occasionally so it doesn't stick to the bottom. Add in the chicken, and cook for two minutes.

4. Ladle the soup and serve topped with cheese.

Nutrition:

Calories: 187.

Protein: 15 Grams.

Fat: 5 Grams.

Carbs: 16 Grams.

Honey Almond Chicken Tenders

Preparation time: 10 minutes.

Cooking Time: 20 Minutes.

Serving: 4.

Ingredients:

- 1 Tablespoon Honey, Raw.
- 1 Tablespoon Dijon Mustard.
- 1 Cup Almonds.
- Sea Salt & Black Pepper to Taste.
- 1 Lb. Chicken Breast Tenders, Boneless & Skinless.

Directions:

1. Start by heating your oven to 425, and then get out a baking sheet. Line it with parchment paper, and then put a cooking rack on it. Spray your cooling rack down with nonstick cooking spray.

2. Get out a bowl and combine your mustard and honey. Season with salt and pepper, and then add in your chicken. Make sure it's well coated and place it to the side.

3. Use a knife and chop your almonds. You can also use a food processor. You want them to roughly be the same size as sunflower seeds. Press your chicken into the almonds, and then lay it on your cooking rack.

4. Bake for fifteen to twenty minutes. Your chicken should be cooked all the way through.

Nutrition:

Calories: 263.

Protein: 31 Grams.

Fat: 12 Grams.

Carbs: 9 Grams.

Special Chops

Preparation time: 12 minutes.

Cooking time: 12 minutes.

Servings: 2.

Ingredients:

- 2 Lamb Chops.
- Minced Shallots 2 Tablespoons.
- Balsamic Vinegar, 2 Tablespoons.
- Chicken Broth, 2 Tablespoons.
- Basil, ¼ Teaspoon.
- Rosemary, 1 Teaspoon.

- Thyme, ¼ Teaspoon.
- Salt And Pepper As Needed.
- Extra Virgin Olive Oil, 1 Tablespoon.
- Greek Yogurt, 2 Tablespoons.

Directions:

1. Take a mixing bowl and mix all herbs and yogurt with seasoning.
2. Rub this mixture into the chops completely. Leave them for a few minutes.
3. Heat a skillet over medium heat and cook both sides of the chops well.
4. When tender, brown the shallots on the skillet and add the vinegar and broth.
5. Top the chops with the warm sauce of broth and serve on a platter.

Nutrition:

Calories: 255.

Fat: 13.9g.

Fiber: 0.2g.

Carbs: 5g.

Protein: 14.6g.

Rib Roast

Preparation time: 10 minutes.

Cooking time: 80 minutes.

Servings: 2.

Ingredients:

- Rib Roast, 4 Pounds.
- Salt And Pepper To Taste.
- Garlic, 1 Clove, Minced.
- Extra Virgin Olive Oil, 1 Teaspoon.
- Thyme, ¼ Teaspoon.

Directions:

1. Arrange The Meat In The Roasting Pan.
2. Take A Small Bowl, And Mix The Rest Of The Ingredients.
3. Apply The Mixture To The Meat. Leave For One Hour.
4. Bake That At 500F For 25 Minutes.
5. Then, Bake Again At 325F For 80 Minutes.
6. Serve warm.

Nutrition:

Calories: 562.

Fat: 48g.

Fiber: 0.2g.

Carbs: 1g.

Protein: 29.6g.

Spicy   Lamb   Rounds

Preparation time: 10 minutes.

Cooking time: 12 minutes.

Servings: 2.

Ingredients:

- Ground Lamb, 1 Pound.
- Garlic, 1 Tablespoon, Chopped.
- Mint Leaves, 1 Tablespoon, Chopped.
- Oregano, 1 Tablespoon, Chopped.
- Cilantro, 1 Tablespoon, Chopped.
- Red Pepper, ½ Teaspoon.

- Ground Cumin, ½ Teaspoon.
- Salt and Pepper, ½ Teaspoon Each.
- Feta Cheese, 4 Ounces.
- Extra Virgin Olive Oil As Needed.
- Greek Yogurt, 2 Tablespoons.

Directions:

1. Heat a grill pan over medium heat.
2. Meanwhile, coat the lamb with the yogurt, all the spices, seasoning, and herbs in a bowl.
3. Mix the rest of the ingredients, excluding the feta cheese.
4. Brush the grill pan with cooking oil.
5. Shape the lamb meat into small round cutlets or patties.
6. Grill them, and serve with cheese on top.

Nutrition:

Calories: 478.

Fat: 22.4g.

Fiber: 1.9g.

Carbs: 38g.

Protein: 29.4g.

Prime BBQ

Preparation time: 35 minutes.

Cooking time: 85 minutes.

Servings: 2.

Ingredients:

- Ribs of Your Choice, 2 Pounds.
- Garlic, 1 Teaspoon, Minced.
- Pepper to Taste.
- Salt as Needed.

Directions:

1. Take a large pot and apply salt, pepper, and garlic well to the ribs.
2. Boil the ribs in boiling water.
3. When tender, bake them at 325f for 15 minutes.
4. Cover them in aluminum foil and place a warm coal piece on the foil.
5. Let the ribs absorb the coal smell and taste for one hour.
6. Bake the ribs again.
7. Serve warm.

Nutrition:

Calories: 441.

Fat: 22.2g.

Fiber: 0.7g.

Carbs: 24.5g.

Protein: 33.3g.

Delicious Mutton

Preparation time: 15 minutes.

Cooking time: 25 minutes.

Servings: 2.

Ingredients:

- Water, 1 Tablespoon.
- Soy Sauce, 2 Teaspoons.
- Garlic, 1/8 Teaspoon.
- Beef, 5 Ounces.
- Cornstarch, 2 Teaspoons.
- Broth of Your Choice (E.G., Beef or Chicken), 14 Ounces.

- Broccoli, 1 Cup Florets.
- Extra Virgin Olive Oil, 1 Teaspoon.

Directions:

1. Take a saucepan, and add the oil to warm.
2. Fry the beef strips and sprinkle the water over them. Stir well for some time.
3. Mix soy sauce, garlic, cornstarch, broccoli, and broth with the beef.
4. Let the juices mix with the meat. Leave it on the flame to simmer.
5. Serve when the sauce has thickened.

Nutrition:

Calories: 232.

Fat: 4.9g.

Fiber: 2.6g.

Carbs: 28.7g.

Protein: 17.9g.

Sushi Beef

Preparation time: 12 minutes.

Cooking time: 22 minutes.

Servings: 2.

Ingredients:

- Extra Virgin Olive Oil, 1 Teaspoon.
- Onion, ¼ Cup, Diced.
- Celery, 2 Tablespoons, Diced.
- Mushrooms, 2 Ounces, Chopped.
- Spinach, Fresh, 2 Ounces.
- Stock, ¼ Cup.
- Soy Sauce, 1 Teaspoon.
- Beef, ½ Pound, Sliced.

Directions:

1. Take a wok and the heating oil. Add beef, and stir.
2. Mix the sauce and toss with the veggies and mushrooms when beef is brown.
3. Cook well, and then fold in the spinach.
4. Serve after a couple of minutes.

Nutrition:

Calories: 207.

Fat: 13.4g.

Fiber: 1.6g.

Carbs: 5.5g.

Protein: 16.4g.

Grilled Lemon Chicken

Preparation time: 10 minutes.

Cooking time: 15 minutes.

Servings: 6.

Ingredients:

- 6 Ounces Boneless Skinless Chicken Breasts.
- 1/4 Cup Olive Oil.
- 1/4 Cup Lemon Juice plus the Zest for the Lemons.
- 2 Teaspoons Oregano.

- 4 Garlic Cloves Pressed.
- 1/2 Teaspoon Salt.
- 1/4 Teaspoon Pepper.
- Parsley or Cilantro for Serving.
- Lemon Wedges for Serving.

Directions:

1. Pat chicken dry and pound chicken if some parts are too thick. Combine the olive oil, lemon juice, oregano, garlic, salt, and pepper in a bowl or resealable freezer bag. Add chicken and toss well to combine. Marinate for at least 30 minutes.

2. Preheat grill or grill pan to medium-high heat. Place chicken on the grill for 5-7 minutes. Use tongs to flip over and cook until juices run dry, approximately 5-7 more minutes. Discard extra marinade.

3. Remove chicken from the grill. Sprinkle with parsley and serve with lemon wedges and vegetables, if desired.

Nutrition:

Calories: 216kcal.

Carbohydrates: 2g

Protein: 24g.

Fat: 12g.

Saturated Fat: 2g.
Cholesterol: 72mg.

Quick Chicken Salad Wraps

Preparation time: 10 minutes.

Cooking time: 10 minutes.

Servings: 6.

Ingredients:

- 2 (10 Ounces) Cans Chunk Chicken, Drained and Flaked.
- ¼ Cup Chopped Onion.
- ¼ Cup Mayonnaise.
- 4 Tablespoons Fresh Salsa.
- Salt and Pepper To Taste.
- 6 (10 inches) Flour Tortillas.
- 12 Lettuce Leaves.

Directions:

1. In a small bowl combine the chicken, onion, mayonnaise, salsa, salt, and pepper. Mix.
2. Line each tortilla with two lettuce leaves, then divide the chicken salad mixture evenly among each tortilla and roll up, or 'wrap'.

Nutrition:

Per Serving: 464 Calories.
Protein: 27.2g.
Carbohydrates: 42.5g.
Fat: 14.8g.
Cholesterol: 61.4mg.
Sodium: 933.7mg.

Spiced Roast Chicken

Preparation time: 15 minutes.

Cooking time: 1 hour.

Servings: 8.

Ingredients:

- 1 (3 Pound) Whole Chicken.
- 1 Tablespoon Olive Oil.
- ¼ Teaspoon Salt.
- ¼ Teaspoon Ground Black Pepper.
- ¼ Teaspoon Dried Oregano.
- ¼ Teaspoon Dried Basil.
- ¼ Teaspoon Paprika.
- 1/8 Teaspoon Cayenne Pepper.

Directions:

1. Preheat oven to 450 degrees F (230 degrees C).

2. Rinse chicken thoroughly inside and out under cold running water and remove all fat. Pat dry with paper towels.

3. Put the chicken into a small baking pan. Rub with olive oil. Mix the salt, pepper, oregano, basil, paprika, and cayenne pepper and sprinkle over the chicken.

4. Roast the chicken in the preheated oven for 20 minutes. Lower the oven to 400 degrees F (205 degrees C) and continue roasting to a minimum internal temperature of 165 degrees F (74 degrees C), about 40 minutes more. Let cool 10 to 15 minutes and serve.

Nutrition:

Per	Serving:	229	Calories.
Protein:			23g.
Carbohydrates:			0.2g.
Fat:			14.5g.
Cholesterol:			72.8mg.

Sodium: 142.7mg.

Coconut Chicken Tenders

Preparation time: 15 minutes.

Cooking time: 1 hour.

Servings: 8.

Ingredients:

- 1-Pound Chicken Tenderloins Or Chicken Breasts, Cut Into Strips.
- 1/2 Cup Flour.
- 1/2 Teaspoon Chili Powder
- 1/2 Teaspoon Salt.
- 1/4 Teaspoon Pepper.

- 2 Eggs.
- 2 Tablespoons Water or Milk or Milk.
- 2/3 Cup Shredded Sweetened Coconut Flakes.
- 2/3 Cup Panko Bread Crumbs.
- Oil for Frying See Notes for Alternate Baking Method.
- Sea Salt Flakes for Garnish, Optional.
- Sweet Chili Sauce for Serving.

Directions:

1. First, get out four wide, shallow bowls. In the first bowl, whisk together the flour, chili powder, salt, and pepper.

2. In a second bowl, whisk together the eggs and water (or milk).

3. Fill a third bowl with coconut flakes, and a fourth bowl with panko bread crumbs.

4. Toss chicken tenders first in the flour, then in the egg wash, followed by the coconut flakes, and ending with the bread crumbs. Be sure to coat each chicken tender thoroughly with each step.

5. For frying (see notes for baking method) fill a large skillet with 1 inch of oil. Bring to temperature over medium heat.

6. Use tongs to transfer chicken tenders into the oil (do not crowd the pan, fry in batches if you need to). Cook for 2-3 minutes, then turn chicken tenders over and cook

another 3-4 minutes until golden brown and chicken is cooked through.

7. Repeat with remaining chicken tenders as needed. Allow cooling slightly on a wire cooling rack over paper towels.
8. Garnish with sea salt flakes if desired and serve warm with sweet chili dipping sauce.

Nutrition:

Calories: 161.

Protein: 14.04g.

Carbohydrates: 0.2g.

Fat: 5.68g.

Cholesterol: 184mg

Sodium: 798mg.

Baked Teriyaki Turkey Meatballs

Preparation time: 20 minutes.

Cooking time: 30 minutes.

Servings: 30.

Ingredients:

THE SAUCE:

- 1/3 Cup Rice Vinegar.
- 1/4 Cup Agave Nectar.

- 1/3 Cup Water.
- 1/4 Cup Soya Sauce.
- 1/4 Cup Canola Oil.
- 1 Tablespoon All-Purpose Flour.
- 2 Teaspoons Minced Fresh Ginger.
- 2 Minced Garlic Cloves.
- 2 Teaspoons Toasted Sesame Seeds.

THE MEATBALLS:
- 1 1/4 Pounds Ground Turkey Meat Preferably Not Extra-Lean.
- 1/2 Medium Yellow Onion Grated.
- 2 Cloves Garlic Minced.
- 2 Teaspoons Grated Ginger
- 1/4 Cup Chopped Italian Parsley.
- 3/4 Teaspoon Five-Spice Powder.
- 1 Egg.
- 1/4 Cup Plus 2 Tablespoons Dried Breadcrumbs.
- 1 Teaspoon Kosher Salt.
- 1/2 Teaspoons Freshly Ground Black Pepper.

Directions:
THE SAUCE:

1. In a small saucepan, combine rice vinegar, agave nectar, water, soya sauce, 1/4 cup canola oil, ginger, garlic, flour, and sesame seeds.
2. Whisk the sauce together and place over medium heat. Simmer until the sauce is slightly thickened, 8 to 10 minutes. Keep warm.

THE MEATBALLS:

1. Preheat the oven to 350 degrees F. Thoroughly coat a large baking sheet with cooking spray.
2. In a large bowl, combine ground turkey, grated onion, garlic, ginger, parsley, five-spice powder, egg, breadcrumbs, salt, and pepper.
3. Mix well to combine. Using a 2-tablespoon portion of the turkey mixture, form meatballs by rolling between the palms of your hands. Place the meatballs on the prepared baking sheet, spacing evenly.
4. Bake until the meatballs are firm to the touch and cooked for about 15 minutes.
5. Brush the meatballs liberally with the sauce. Return to the oven for 5 minutes. Serve immediately.
6. These can be served over rice or as hors d'oeuvres. Either way, serve with the extra sauce.

Nutrition:

Calories: 62kcal.

Carbohydrates: 3g.

Protein: 4g.

Fat: 4g.

Saturated   Fat: 1g.

Cholesterol: 19mg.

Grilled Chicken and Zucchini Kebabs

Preparation time: 10 minutes.

Cooking time: 12 minutes.

Servings: 5.

Ingredients:

- 2 Boneless Chicken Breasts Cut Into 1-Inch Pieces.
- 2 Medium Zucchini Sliced Into Thick Rounds.

- 1 Large Red Onion Cut into 1-Inch Pieces.
- 2 Large Lemons.
- 3 Cloves Garlic Minced.
- 1 Tablespoon Chopped Fresh Thyme.
- 1 Tablespoon Chopped Fresh Rosemary.
- ¼ Cup Bertolli® 100% Pure Olive Oil.
- 1 Teaspoon Kosher Salt.
- ½ Teaspoon Freshly Ground Pepper.

Directions:

1. Place the chicken pieces in a large Ziploc bag or bowl. Place the zucchini and red onion in a separate Ziploc bag or bowl. Set aside.

2. Zest one of the lemons and place the zest in a medium bowl. Juice both lemons and add to the lemon zest. Add the minced garlic, thyme, rosemary, olive oil, salt, and pepper. Whisk the marinade together. Pour half of the marinade into the freezer bag or bowl with the chicken pieces and pour the other half in the freezer bag or bowl with the zucchini and onion. Let marinate for 30 minutes or up to 4 hours in the refrigerator.

3. When ready to grill, make the kebabs. Alternate chicken, zucchini, and onion on skewers. Discard any remaining marinade.

4. Lightly brush the grill with olive oil and preheat to medium heat.

5. Grill chicken kebabs, turning often so each side browns and has light grill marks, about 10-12 minutes or until chicken is cooked through. Serve immediately.

6. Note-If using wooden skewers, soak them in water before using them. If using metal skewers, no prep is necessary.

Nutrition:

Calories:	78kcal.
Carbohydrates:	6.09g.
Protein:	1.62g.
Fat:	5.54g.
Saturated Fat:	0.85g.
Cholesterol: 7mg.	

Gyro Burgers with Tahini Sauce

Preparation time: 10 minutes.

Cooking time: 12 minutes.

Servings: 4.

Ingredients:

- 1-Pound Extra-Lean Ground Beef.
- 1 Teaspoon Greek Seasoning.
- 4 Pita Rounds.
- 4 Lettuce Leaves.
- 8 Large Tomato Slices.

- 4 Thin Red Onion Slices.
- Tahini Sauce.
- 1/4 Cup Feta Cheese.

Directions:

1. Combine beef and seasoning. Shape into 4 patties.
2. Grill, covered with grill lid, over medium-high heat (350° to 400°) 5 to 6 minutes on each side or until beef is no longer pink.
3. Cut off 2 inches of bread from 1 side of each pita round, forming a pocket. Line each with 1 lettuce leaf, 2 tomato slices, and 1 red onion slice. Add burger. Drizzle each with 2 tablespoons Tahini Sauce, and sprinkle with 1 tablespoon cheese.

Nutrition:

Calories:		297kcal.
Carbohydrates:		2.81g.
Protein:		29.42g.
Fat:		17.83g.
Saturated	Fat:	7.41g.
Cholesterol: 105mg.		

Garlicky Tomato Chicken Casserole

Preparation Time: 5 minutes

Cooking Time: 50 minutes

Servings: 4

Ingredients:

- 4 chicken breasts
- 2 tomatoes, sliced
- 1 can diced tomatoes

- 2 cloves of garlic, chopped
- 1 shallot, chopped
- 1 bay leaf
- 1 thyme sprig
- ½ cup dry white wine
- ½ cup chicken stock
- Salt and pepper to taste

Directions:

1. Combine the chicken and the remaining ingredients in a deep-dish baking pan.
2. Adjust the taste with salt and pepper and cover the pot with a lid or aluminum foil.
3. Cook in the preheated oven at 330F for 40 minutes.
4. Serve the casserole warm.

Nutrition:

Calories: 313 kcal

Fat: 8g

Protein: 47g

Carbohydrates: 6g

Chicken Cacciatore

Preparation Time: 5 minutes

Cooking Time: 45 minutes

Servings: 6

Ingredients:

- 2 tbsp extra virgin olive oil
- 6 chicken thighs
- 1 sweet onion, chopped
- 2 garlic cloves, minced
- 2 red bell peppers, cored and diced
- 2 carrots, diced

- 1 rosemary sprig
- 1 thyme sprig
- 4 tomatoes, peeled and diced
- ½ cup tomato juice
- ¼ cup dry white wine
- 1 cup chicken stock
- 1 bay leaf
- Salt and pepper to taste

Directions:

1. Heat the oil in a heavy saucepan.
2. Cook chicken on all sides until golden.
3. Stir in the onion and garlic and cook for 2 minutes.
4. Stir in the rest of the ingredients and season with salt and pepper.
5. Cook on low heat for 30 minutes.
6. Serve the chicken cacciatore warm and fresh.

Nutrition:

Calories: 363 kcal

Fat: 14g

Protein: 42g

Carbohydrates: 9g

Herbed Roasted Chicken Breasts

Preparation Time: 5 minutes

Cooking Time: 50 minutes

Servings: 4

Ingredients

- 2 tbsp extra virgin olive oil
- 2 tbsp chopped parsley
- 2 tbsp chopped cilantro
- 1 tsp dried oregano
- 1 tsp dried basil
- 2 tbsp lemon juice

- Salt and pepper to taste
- 4 chicken breasts

Directions:

1. Combine the oil, parsley, cilantro, oregano, basil, lemon juice, salt and pepper in a bowl.
2. Spread this mixture over the chicken and rub it well into the meat.
3. Place in a deep-dish baking pan and cover with aluminum foil.
4. Cook in the preheated oven at 350F for 20 minutes then remove the foil and cook for 25 additional minutes.
5. Serve the chicken warm and fresh with your favorite side dish.

Nutrition:

Calories: 330 kcal

Fat: 15g

Protein: 40.7g

Carbohydrates: 1g

Minted Lamb with a Couscous Salad Recipe

Preparation Time: 5 minutes

Cooking Time: 10 minutes

Servings: 2

Ingredients:

- 75g couscous
- ½ chicken stock cube made up to 125ml
- 30g pack fresh flat-leaf parsley, chopped
- 3 mint sprigs, leaves picked and chopped
- 1 tbsp olive oil

- 200g   pack frozen BBQ minted lamb leg steaks, defrosted
- 200g salad tomatoes, chopped
- ¼ cucumber, chopped
- 1 spring onion, chopped
- pinch of ground cumin
- ½ lemon, zested and juiced
- 50g reduced-fat salad cheese

Direction:

1. Put the couscous in a heatproof bowl and pour over the stock. Cover and set aside for 10 mins, then fluff with a fork and stir in the herbs.

2. Meanwhile, rub a little oil over the lamb steaks and season. Cook to pack instructions, then slice.

3. Mix the tomatoes, cucumber and spring onion into the couscous with the remaining oil, cumin, and lemon zest and juice. Crumble over the salad cheese and serve with the lamb.

Nutrition:

Calories: 337 kcal

Fat: 17.38g

Protein: 31.57g

Carbohydrates: 15.14g

Mongolian Beef

Preparation Time: 10 minutes

Cooking Time: 25 minutes

Serving: 4

Ingredients:

- 1-pound flank steak
- 1/4 cup cornstarch
- 1/4 cup canola oil
- 2 tsp fresh ginger, minced
- 1 tbsp garlic, minced

- 1/3 cup lite soy sauce, low sodium
- 1/3 cup water
- 1/2 cup dark brown sugar

Direction:

1. 4 stalks scallions, green parts only, cut into 2-inch pieces
2. Slice the flank steak against the grain (the grain is the length of the steak) the long way 1/4 inch think pieces and add it to a Ziploc bag with the cornstarch.
3. Press the steak around in the bag, making sure each piece is fully coated with cornstarch and leave it to sit.
4. Add the canola oil to a large frying pan and heat on medium-high heat.
5. Add the steak, shaking off any excess cornstarch, to the pan in a single layer and cook on each side for 1 minute.
6. If you need to cook the steak in batches because your pan isn't big enough do that rather than crowding the pan you want to get a good sear on the steak and if you crowd the pan your steak with steam instead of sear.
7. When the steak is done, remove it from the pan.
8. Add the ginger and garlic to the pan and sauté for 10-15 seconds.
9. Add the soy sauce, water and dark brown sugar to the pan and let it come to a boil.
10. Add the steak back in and let the sauce thicken for 20-30 seconds.

11. The cornstarch we used on the steak should thicken the sauce, if you find it isn't thickening enough add 1 tablespoon of cornstarch to 1 tablespoon of cold water and stir to dissolve the cornstarch and add it to the pan.
12. Add the green onions, stir to combine everything, and cook for a final 20-30 seconds.
13. Serve immediately.

Nutrition:

Calories: 433 kcal

Calories: 433g

Carbohydrates: 37g

Protein: 27g

Fat: 20g

Saturated Fat: 3g

Cholesterol: 68mg,

Char-Grilled Steak

Preparation Time: 1 hour 40 minutes

Cooking Time: 16 minutes

Servings: 5

Ingredients:

- 1 tsp salt plus more for seasoning
- 1 tsp cornstarch
- 4 rib-eye steaks about 1 1/2" thick, around 1 pound each
- pepper

Direction:

1. In a small bowl, combine the salt and cornstarch.
2. Pat the steaks dry and rub with the salt mixture.
3. Place the steaks on a wire rack and chill in the freezer for 30 minutes to 1 hour.
4. Meanwhile, build a fire on your charcoal grill and clean the grate for when those steaks are ready to go.
5. Season the steaks with pepper.
6. Grill for 4 to 8 minutes per side (for your desired doneness – 4 is my lucky number).
7. Remove from the grill and tent with foil. Allow resting for 5 minutes before serving.
8. To serve, slice thin on an angle against the grain

Nutrition:

Calories: 472 kcal

Fat: 32g

Carbohydrates: 1g

Protein: 46g

Meatballs with Salad

Preparation Time: 20 minutes

Cooking Time: 15 minutes

Servings: 4

Ingredients:

For Meatballs:

- 1-pound lean ground turkey
- 1 cup frozen chopped spinach, thawed and squeezed
- ½ cup feta cheese, crumbled
- ½ tsp dried oregano
- Salt and ground black pepper, as required
- 2 tbsp olive oil

For Salad:

- 4 cups fresh baby spinach
- 1 cup cherry tomatoes, halved

Directions:

1. **For meatballs**: place all ingredients except for oil in a bowl and mix until well blended.
2. Make 12 equal-sized meatballs from the mixture.
3. In a large non-stick pan, heat the olive oil over medium heat and cook the meatballs for about 10-15 minutes or until done completely, flipping occasionally.
4. With a slotted spoon, place the meatballs onto a plate.
5. **Meanwhile, for salad**: in a large salad bowl, add all ingredients and toss to coat well.
6. Divide meatballs and salad onto serving plates and serve.

Nutrition:

Calories: 289 kcal

Fat: 19g

Carbohydrates: 4g

Fiber: 1.5g

Sugar: 2.1g

Protein: 26.4g

Beef Burgers

Preparation Time: 15 minutes

Cooking Time: 12 minutes

Servings: 4

Ingredients:

For Burgers:

- 1-pound lean ground beef
- 1 cup fresh baby spinach leaves, chopped
- ½ of small yellow onion, chopped
- ¼ cup sun-dried tomatoes, chopped
- 1 egg, beaten
- ¼ cup feta cheese, crumbled

- Salt and ground black pepper, as required
- 2 tbsp olive oil

For Serving:
- 4 cups fresh spinach, torn
- 1 large tomato, sliced

Directions:
1. **For burgers**: In a large bowl, add all ingredients except for oil and mix until well blended.
2. Make 4 equal-sized patties from the mixture.
3. In a pan, heat the oil over medium-high heat and cook the patties for about 5-6 minutes per side or until desired doneness.
4. Divide the spinach and tomato slices and onto serving plates.
5. Top each plate with 1 burger and serve.

Nutrition:

Calories: 244 kcal

Fat: 19g

Carbohydrates: 4.9g

Fiber: 1.7g

Sugar: 2.5g

Protein: 15g

Conclusion

Don't be fooled by the word "diet". You will never be hungry with the Mediterranean diet. Low in fat but flavorful, this healthy way of eating is easy to follow, as well as being a more balanced way of eating. Avoiding dairy and potatoes and the low salt content create leaner, healthier versions of the foods we love. The Mediterranean diet is also richer in phytochemicals, plant chemicals, including antioxidants and anti-inflammatories. Don't forget that good fat is good for you. And contrary to popular opinion, legumes, such as beans and lentils, go well with fish. Welcome to the Mediterranean diet. Remember that a healthy, balanced diet tastes good and keeps you well. Light on meat, rich in vegetables and fruit, the Mediterranean diet has its roots as a traditional diet in the Mediterranean basin. The diet is very tasty, no wonder it is spread all over the world. That is why it is also known as the "healthiest way to eat" and the "Mediterranean diet". Although this book is meat specific, for a proper Mediterranean diet, you should try to eat as many vegetables as possible in your diet to get the nutrients you need, such as vitamins, which you cannot get from many foods. But the Mediterranean diet is not just about vegetables, you should also eat a lot of fish not only to be healthy but to get energy and you should also eat a lot of fruit. Fruits are good for you, but you shouldn't eat them past their expiration date, as they aren't as healthy as they might be after that date. Like vegetables, fruit is especially good because it gives you vitamins that you can't get from many foods. You can buy a lot of fish and seafood and you should try to eat as much fish as you can because it is very healthy. You should try to eat fish every day as it contains Omega 3, a very healthy fat. You should eat non-fat meats such as chicken, turkey or beef, as they contain protein, and your body needs protein to maintain and build muscle cells.

Appendix 1: Measurement Conversion Chart

VOLUME EQUIVALENTS (LIQUID)

US STANDARD	US STANDARD (OUNCES)	METRIC (APPROXIMATE)
2 TABLESPOONS	1 FL. OZ.	30 ML
¼ CUP	2 FL. OZ.	60 ML
½ CUP	4 FL. OZ.	120 ML
1 CUP	8 FL. OZ.	240 ML
1½ CUPS	12 FL. OZ.	355 ML
2 CUPS OR 1 PINT	16 FL. OZ.	475 ML
4 CUPS OR 1 QUART	32 FL. OZ.	1 L
1 GALLON	128 FL. OZ.	4 L

OVEN TEMPERATURES

FAHRENHEIT(F)	CELSIUS (C) (APPROXIMATE)
250°F	120°C
300°F	150°C
325°F	165°C
350°F	180°C
375°F	190°C
400°F	200°C
425°F	220°C
450°F	230°C

VOLUME EQUIVALENTS (DRY)

US STANDARD	METRIC (APPROXIMATE)
⅛ TEASPOON	0.5 ML
¼ TEASPOON	1 ML
½ TEASPOON	2 ML
¾ TEASPOON	4 ML
1 TEASPOON	5 ML
1 TABLESPOON	15 ML
¼ CUP	59 ML
⅓ CUP	79 ML
½ CUP	118 ML
⅔ CUP	156 ML
¾ CUP	177 ML
1 CUP	235 ML
2 CUPS OR 1 PINT	475 ML
3 CUPS	700 ML

4 CUPS OR 1 QUART	1 L

WEIGHT EQUIVALENTS

US STANDARD	METRIC (APPROXIMATE)
½ OUNCE	15 G
1 OUNCE	30 G
2 OUNCES	60 G
4 OUNCES	115 G
8 OUNCES	225 G
12 OUNCES	340 G
16 OUNCES OR 1 POUND	455 G

CPSIA information can be obtained
at www.ICGtesting.com
Printed in the USA
BVHW020434160221
600146BV00020B/18